I0816585

PREHISTORIC LIFE

A WARM, WET WORLD

—THE JURASSIC PERIOD—

by
Dougal Dixon

Ursa Books, an imprint of Bearport Publishing by FlutterBee

Credits
Cover and title page, © dottedyeti/AdobeStock; 3, © Seamless Ahamad/Shutterstock; 4T, © Orla/Shutterstock; 4B, © Capture Wave Media/Shutterstock; 4–5, © Orla/iStock; 5B, © Warren R Schmidt/Shutterstock; 6T, © Michael Rosskothen/Shutterstock; 6M, © SciePro/Shutterstock; 6B, © david.costa.art/Shutterstock; 6–7, © Daniel Eskridge/Shutterstock; 7, © SciePro/Shutterstock; 8–9, © Catmando/Shutterstock; 8, © Warpaint/Shutterstock; 9T, © Abdul_Shakoor/Shutterstock; 9B, © Elenarts/Shutterstock; 10–11, © Mat Edwards; 10M, © Michael Rosskothen/Shutterstock; 10B, © Catmando/Shutterstock; 11, © Catmando/Shutterstock; 12–13, © Petmal/iStockand © Warpaintcobra/iStock; 12T, © INTERFOTO/Alamy Stock Photo; 12B, © Elenarts/Shutterstock; 13, © Elenarts/Shutterstock; 14–15, © rodos studio FERHAT CINAR/Shutterstock; 14T, © rodos studio FERHAT CINAR/Shutterstock; 14B, © Art_rich/Shutterstock; 15, © Catmando/Shutterstock; 16–17, © Mat Edwards; 16, © Nita Yuko/Shutterstock; 17T, © Daniel Eskridge/Shutterstock; 17B, © Vorobiov Oleksii 8/Shutterstock; 18–19, © Catmando/Shutterstock; 18M, © DM7/Shutterstock; 18B, © Catmando/Shutterstock; 19T, © Gwoeii/Shutterstock; 19B, © Michael Rosskothen/Shutterstock; 20–21, © Mat Edwards; 20, © Danny Ye/Shutterstock; 21T, © Michael Rosskothen/Shutterstock; 21B, © Warpaint/Shutterstock; 22–23, © Daniel Eskridge/Shutterstock; 22M, © Radiokafka/Shutterstock; 22B, © Daniel Eskridge/Shutterstock; 23T, © Elenarts/Shutterstock; 23M, © Michael Rosskothen/Shutterstock; 24–25, © Elenarts/Shutterstock; 24M, © YuRi Photolife/Shutterstock; 24B, © Igor Karasi/Shutterstock; 25, © Warpaint/Shutterstock; 26–27, © Mat Edwards; 26T, © lego 19861111/Shutterstock; 26M, © Warpaint/Shutterstock; 26B, © Warpaint/Shutterstock; 27, © kamomeen/Shutterstock; 28–29, © Dotted Yeti/Shutterstock; 28M, © Michael Rosskothen/Shutterstock; 28B, © Herschel Hoffmeyer/Shutterstock; 29T, © Arcturus Image Bank; 29M, © Arcturus Image Bank; 30–31, © Mohamad Haghani/Stocktrek Images/Getty Images; 30T, © Guido Vermeulen-Perdaen/Alamy Stock Photo; 30B, © Jim West/Alamy Stock Photo; 31, © kamomeen/Shutterstock; 32–33, © Mohamad Haghani/Alamy Stock Photo; 32T, © Science Photo Library/ Alamy Stock Photo; 32B, © Science History Images/Alamy Stock Photo; 33, © 3dMediSphere/Shutterstock; 34–35, © ROGER HARRIS/Science Source; 34T, © UPI/Alamy Stock Photo; 34B, © Public Domain/Wikimedia Commons; 35, © Public Domain/Wikimedia Commons; 36–37, © Dotted Yeti/Shutterstock; 36T, © Public Domain/Wikimedia Commons; 36B, © Universal Images Group North America LLC/Alamy Stock Photo; 37, © Dotted Yeti/Shutterstock; 38–39, © Michael Rosskothen/Shutterstock; 38T, © Stocktrek Images, Inc./Alamy Stock Photo; 38B, © Science History Images/Alamy Stock Photo; 39, © 3dMediSphere/Shutterstock; 40–41, © MattL_Images/Shutterstock; 40T, © Mark Stevenson/Stocktrek Images/Getty Images; 40B, © Jon G. Fuller/VWPics/Alamy Stock Photo; 41, © 3dMediSphere/Shutterstock; 42–43, © paleontologist natural/Shutterstock; 42T, © William Mullins/Alamy Stock Photo; 42B, © Anthony Romilio, Ron Park, Wes Nichols, and Owen Jackson/Historical Biology; 43, © Felix Choo/Alamy Stock Photo; 44B, © Mohamad Haghani/Stocktrek Images/Getty Images; 45T, © INTERFOTO/ Alamy Stock Photo; 45B, © Stocktrek Images, Inc./Alamy Stock Photo; 47, © Michael Rosskothen/Shutterstock.

Bearport Publishing Company Product Development Team
Kayla Eggert, Theresa Emminizer, Kim Jones, Allison Juda, Cole Nelson, Naomi Reich, Steve Scheluchin, Tiana Tran

Statement on Usage of Generative Artificial Intelligence
Bearport Publishing remains committed to publishing high-quality nonfiction books. Therefore, we restrict the use of generative AI to ensure accuracy of all text and visual components pertaining to a book's subject. See BearportPublishing.com for details.

Library of Congress Cataloging-in-Publication Data is available at www.loc.gov or upon request from the publisher.

ISBN: 979-8-89577-743-5 (hardcover)
ISBN: 979-8-89577-751-0 (ebook)

For more information, write to Bearport Publishing, 5357 Penn Avenue South, Minneapolis, MN 55419. Printed in the United States of America.

Contents

Jurassic Life

The Jurassic Period began more than 200 million years ago. During this time, the supercontinent called Pangaea split into smaller land masses and oceans flowed into the areas between. The climate became subtropical and humid, and this caused new forms of life to appear across the planet. Dominant among life on the planet at this time were the dinosaurs—some of the largest land animals to ever live.

The Age of Dinosaurs

The Jurassic is one of three periods that made up the age of the dinosaurs. In these three periods, huge long-necked sauropods and smaller armored dinosaurs fed on plants. Meanwhile, fierce predators, such as *Allosaurus*, were on the hunt for meat.

Sharks first appeared during the Devonian Period 380 million years ago.

Ocean Life

Though ocean life was not as diverse as in previous times, Jurassic seas still teemed with life. Corals and sponges grew into reefs inhabited by bony fish and spiral-shelled ammonites. These all became food for larger marine animals, such as ichthyosaurs, crocodiles, and sharks.

Cycads look a bit like modern palm trees, but they are not related.

Jurassic Plants

About 20 percent of all plants in the Jurassic Period were cycads. These tropical plants were probably a major source of food for herbivores at the time. They were also among the first plants to be pollinated by insects.

Liopleurodon

Many of the largest animals to ever live walked and swam on Earth during the Jurassic Period. In the oceans, giant sea reptiles ruled the waves. The biggest and fiercest of these swimmers were the plesiosaurs.

Two Types of Plesiosaurs

There were two types of plesiosaurs: plesiosauroids and pliosauroids. One of the biggest of the pliosauroids was *Liopleurodon*. Like a modern sperm whale, *Liopleurodon* roamed the oceans of the world hunting for food. With its long jaws and sharp teeth, it fed on big fish, squid-like cephalopods, and even other swimming reptiles.

The teeth and jaws of *Liopleurodon* were strong enough to attack the biggest animals in the ocean.

Liopleurodon was a typical pliosauroid.

What's the Difference?

The two types of plesiosaur are easy to tell apart. Pliosauroids had big heads with long jaws. These big heads were separated from their bodies by short, thick necks. Meanwhile, plesiosauroids had tiny heads, with jaws full of sharp teeth. Their heads were separated from their bodies by long necks.

Cryptoclidus, with its long neck and short head, was a typical plesiosauroid.

DID YOU KNOW? The name *Liopleurodon* means smooth-sided teeth. For years, the only fossils we had of this creature were of its teeth.

Geosaurus

In the Jurassic Period, one branch of the crocodiles took to the seas. These ocean crocodiles were called the thalattosuchians, and there were two families of these crocodiles. One was the teleosauroids, which kept their basic crocodile shape. The other was the metriorhynchoids, which were more highly adapted to life in the ocean.

Adapted to Sea Life

Geosaurus was a typical metriorhynchoid. It had paddles instead of legs and a fishlike fin on the end of its tail. It never ventured out onto land. Like the other sea reptiles of the Jurassic Period, such as the ichthyosaurs and the plesiosaurs, *Geosaurus*'s ancestors had given up life on land altogether.

Geosaurus may have hunted by suction. It may have opened its jaws so suddenly that water was sucked into the mouth, carrying prey with it.

Dakosaurus, a metriorhynchoid that was 16 ft. (5 m) long with a huge head, was nicknamed Godzilla when its fossils were first found.

The biggest species of *Geosaurus* took over from *Liopleurodon* as the apex marine predators at the end of the Jurassic.

Land and Sea

The other group of thalattosuchians, the teleosauroids, would have been able to spend some time on land. They still had legs, feet, and toes, although these were very short and were held tight to the sides of the body while swimming in the sea. With their long, narrow jaws, they looked a bit like the modern gharial crocodile.

Statues of *Teleosaurus* were built for the first prehistoric theme park, which was located in London, England. They were unveiled in 1854.

Geosaurus had smooth skin without the bony plates we see on modern crocodiles.

CAMBRIAN | ORDOVICIAN | SILURIAN | DEVONIAN | CARBONIFEROUS | PERMIAN | TRIASSIC | JURASSIC (150 MYA) | CRETACEOUS | CENOZOIC

Name: *Geosaurus* (*jee*-oh-SORE-us)

Superorder: Crocodylomorphia

Length: Up to 10 ft. (3 m)

Weight: Up to 250 pounds (110 kg)

ANIMAL PROFILE

DID YOU KNOW? Different species of *Geosaurus* had different-sized teeth depending on what they ate.

Rhamphorhynchus

After the gliding reptiles of the Triassic and before birds appeared, the skies belonged to flying reptiles called pterosaurs. These were not dinosaurs, even though they lived during the same era. Pterosaurs ruled the skies from late Triassic times until the great extinction at the end of the Cretaceous Period.

Like all pterosaurs, the wing of *Rhamphorhynchus*, was held out by an enormous fourth finger. These finger bones were as long as arm bones.

Wing Fingers

Pterosaurs were active, warm-blooded flying reptiles, with furry bodies and leathery wings that were supported by a very long, strong fourth finger. The earlier types, such as *Rhamphorhynchus*, had long tails and narrow wings. Later types had broader wings and short tails. Like modern birds, they had different-shaped heads and jaws depending on what they ate. *Rhamphorhynchus* had a long, narrow head perfect for hunting fish.

While on the ground, many pterosaurs walked on all fours. They took to the air in a jump. We can tell this from fossil footprints.

CAMBRIAN	ORDOVICIAN	SILURIAN	DEVONIAN	CARBONIFEROUS	PERMIAN	TRIASSIC	JURASSIC	CRETACEOUS	CENOZOIC
							150 MYA		

Name: *Rhamphorhynchus* (*ram*-foh-RINK-us)
Order: Pterosauria
Wingspan: Up to 33 ft. (10 m)
Weight: Up to 2 lb. (0.9 kg)

ANIMAL PROFILE

Two Types

The two types of pterosaur were rhamphorhynchoids and pterodactyloids. The rhamphorhynchoids came first and were around until the end of the Jurassic Period. They were replaced by the pterodactyloids. By the end of the Cretaceous Period, pterodactyloids became the biggest ever flying animals.

DID YOU KNOW? The best fossils of *Rhamphorhynchus* have been found in southern Germany. On some, even the skin of the wing has been fossilized.

Pterodactylus

Pterodactylus was the first pterosaur to be discovered. Its fossils were originally found in the 1700s. Since then, paleontologists have discovered more than 150 different species of the flying reptiles. Some were small enough to fit in a person's hand, while others had wingspans as large as a fighter jet.

Built to Fly

Pterodactylus had long arms and hand bones. It had smaller teeth and a shorter tail than other pterosaurs. Its large wings were made of leathery skin and shaped like sails. *Pterodactylus* could flap these wings to fly or hold them still to glide on the wind.

Unlike other pterosaurs, whose wings were supported by a finger bone, *Pterodactylus* had a long hand bone that extended from its palm and supported its wing.

Although pterosaurs were reptiles, their bones had similar structures to today's birds.

Hollow Bones

Solid bones would have made *Pterodactylus* and other pterosaurs too heavy to get off the ground. Luckily, the pterosaurs had evolved bones shaped like hollow tubes, making them lightweight and flexible. Structures inside the bones also made them very strong.

CAMBRIAN	ORDOVICIAN	SILURIAN	DEVONIAN	CARBONIFEROUS	PERMIAN	TRIASSIC	JURASSIC	CRETACEOUS	CENOZOIC
							160 MYA		

Name: *Pterodactylus* (*teh*-roe-DACK-till-us)
Order: Pterosauria
Length: Up to 3.3 ft. (1 m)
Weight: Up to 100 lb. (45 kg)

ANIMAL PROFILE

DID YOU KNOW? At first, some scientists thought that *Pterodactylus* was an ocean animal that used its wings like flippers.

Coelophysis

By the start of the Jurassic Period, dinosaurs were developing into the different types that would walk the land until the end of the Cretaceous Period. There were the sauropods, the ornithischians, and the theropods.

Nimble Hunter

Most of the small, carnivorous theropods of the late Triassic and early Jurassic looked like *Coelophysis*. They had small, slim bodies, long running legs, heads held out at the front on long necks, and grasping hands. Although *Coelophysis* itself was found in North America, the fossils of very similar theropods have been found in South Africa.

Flood Victims

The most famous *Coelophysis* fossils were found in New Mexico, where a whole pack of them had perished in a flood and their skeletons were perfectly preserved. Usually, dinosaur fossils consist of only scattered pieces of bone. A full dinosaur skeleton, with the bones still joined together, is very rare.

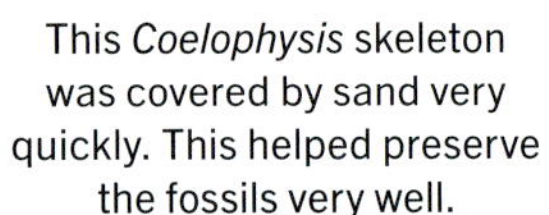

This *Coelophysis* skeleton was covered by sand very quickly. This helped preserve the fossils very well.

CAMBRIAN	ORDOVICIAN	SILURIAN	DEVONIAN	CARBONIFEROUS	PERMIAN	TRIASSIC	JURASSIC	CRETACEOUS	CENOZOIC
						215 MYA			

Name: *Coelophysis* (*see*-loh-FISE-iss)
Clade: Theropoda
Length: Up to 10 ft. (3 m)
Weight: Up to 50 lb. (23 kg)

ANIMAL PROFILE

Some paleontologists believe *Coelophysis* lived in herds. Others think they lived alone. These scientists say their fossils are sometimes found together where a flood swept all of the bodies into one place.

Coelophysis lived on riverbanks in open, arid plains that were periodically flooded.

DID YOU KNOW? A skull fossil of *Coelophysis* was taken into space on a shuttle in 1998.

Dilophosaurus

As the Jurassic Period continued, more and more theropods appeared. They all had a similar shape: they walked on two legs, had mouthfuls of teeth in heads held out at the front, and balanced their bodies with heavy tails.

Meat Eaters Get Bigger

Dilophosaurus was one of the earliest of the big theropods. It was not as huge as the larger dinosaurs to come, but it was certainly the fiercest animal of its time. With its sharp teeth and strong claws, it was built to attack animals even bigger than itself. It would also hunt smaller things and even eat animals that had already died.

The teeth of *Dilophosaurus* were longer and more bladelike on the upper jaw than on the lower jaw.

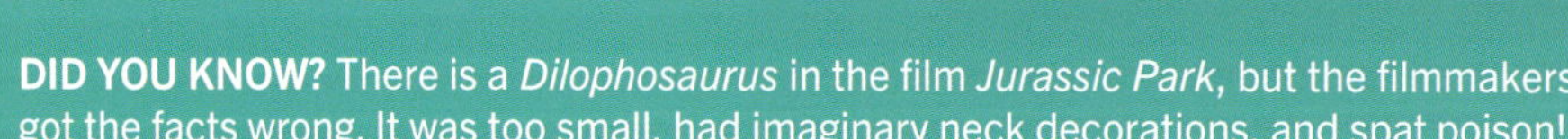

DID YOU KNOW? There is a *Dilophosaurus* in the film *Jurassic Park*, but the filmmakers got the facts wrong. It was too small, had imaginary neck decorations, and spat poison!

Name: *Dilophosaurus* (dy-*loff*-oh-SORE-us)
Clade: Theropoda
Length: Up to 23 ft. (7 m)
Weight: Up to 880 lb. (400 kg)

Show-Off!

Dilophosaurus had two crests running down the top of its head. These were too thin to have been weapons of any sort. They may have been used for display—to show off to rivals or to attract mates. They would probably have been patterned in bright hues.

Dilophosaurus had a lightly built skull. The front part was articulated so that it could twitch, probably to grab small animals out of rock crevices.

Yangchuanosaurus

The really big meat-eating theropods of the Jurassic Period are the carnosaurs. They ranged from the enormous *Allosaurus* of North America and the huge *Carcharodontosaurus* of Africa to the great *Yangchuanosaurus* of China. The long-necked, plant-eating sauropods of the time were their main prey.

Dragon from China

Yangchuanosaurus, like the other carnosaurs, used its strong claws and its vicious teeth for killing. It ran at great speeds powered by the huge muscles of its hind legs. Its clawed hands could sink into the flesh of its prey. And the muscles of its neck could help it close its mouth with enormous force. Then, the bladelike teeth could rip out chunks of meat.

Yangchuanosaurus **had several little horns over its eyes and a ridge of bone on its nose.**

The sharp teeth of *Yangchuanosaurus* regrew and were replaced as they wore out.

Another carnosaur, *Cryolophosaurus*, had a tall crest above its eyes. Its fossils were found in Antarctica.

Carnosaurs may have hunted in packs to kill the biggest animals they could.

A Mysterious Animal

In 1824, the carnosaur *Megalosaurus* became the first dinosaur to have been discovered and named. Before this, nobody knew what a dinosaur looked like. The only fossils people found were those of a jawbone with teeth and some hip bones. They were thought to have belonged to some kind of giant lizard. Scientists imagined that it walked on all fours.

A statue of *Megalosaurus*, as it was then thought to have looked, stands in the grounds of Crystal Palace Park in London, England.

CAMBRIAN	ORDOVICIAN	SILURIAN	DEVONIAN	CARBONIFEROUS	PERMIAN	TRIASSIC	JURASSIC	CRETACEOUS	CENOZOIC
							159 MYA		

Name: *Yangchuanosaurus* (yang-*chwan*-oh-SORE-us)
Order: Theropoda
Length: Up to 33 ft. (10 m)
Weight: Up to 3.3 tn. (3 t)

ANIMAL PROFILE

DID YOU KNOW? The first skeleton of *Yangchuanosaurus* was found in 1977 by workers building a dam in China.

Diplodocus

The biggest of the Jurassic plant eaters were the long-necked sauropods. In fact, sauropods were the biggest land animals ever. In Jurassic times, they developed into two major groups: the diplodocids, which were long and low; and the macronarians, which were tall, but not as long. The most famous of the diplodocids was *Diplodocus* itself.

Dinosaur Celebrity

An almost complete fossil of *Diplodocus* was unearthed in 1899 during an expedition funded by Scottish-American steel tycoon Andrew Carnegie. Once the skeleton was assembled in his museum in Pittsburgh, Pennsylvania, Carnegie was so pleased with it that he had plaster casts made of all 292 bones. He sent copies of the skeleton to the museums of several capital cities throughout the world. As a result, in the early twentieth century, *Diplodocus* was the best known of all dinosaurs.

The skull of *Diplodocus* was as big as that of a horse. But its head was small compared with its body.

DID YOU KNOW? A partial skeleton of a *Diplodocus* that may have been 110 ft. (33 m) long was found in 1991.

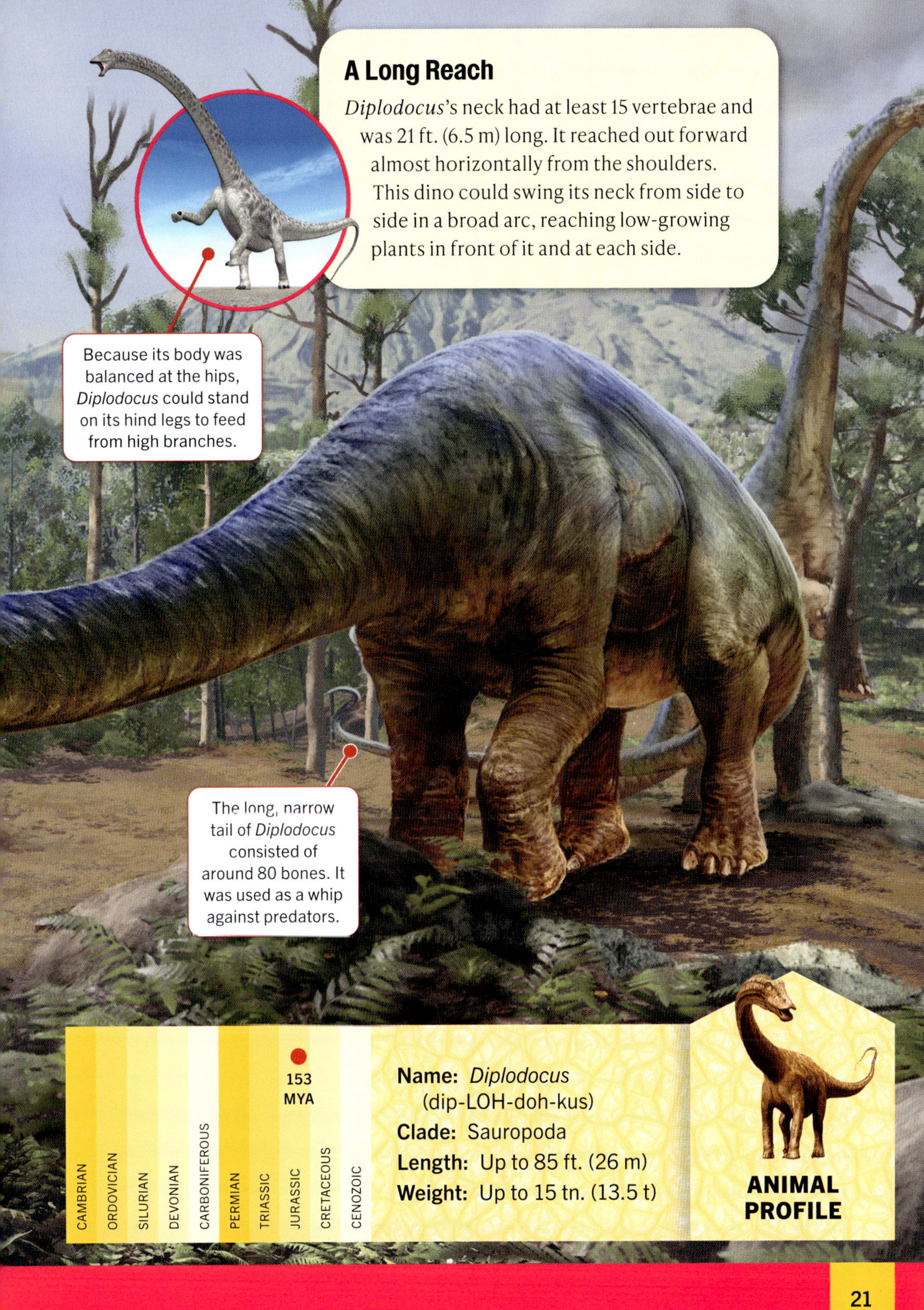

A Long Reach

Diplodocus's neck had at least 15 vertebrae and was 21 ft. (6.5 m) long. It reached out forward almost horizontally from the shoulders. This dino could swing its neck from side to side in a broad arc, reaching low-growing plants in front of it and at each side.

CAMBRIAN | ORDOVICIAN | SILURIAN | DEVONIAN | CARBONIFEROUS | PERMIAN | TRIASSIC | JURASSIC | CRETACEOUS | CENOZOIC

153 MYA

Name: *Diplodocus* (dip-LOH-doh-kus)
Clade: Sauropoda
Length: Up to 85 ft. (26 m)
Weight: Up to 15 tn. (13.5 t)

ANIMAL PROFILE

Brachiosaurus

The second sauropod group were the macronarians. While diplodocids had long bodies, macronarians were remarkably tall. Unusually for dinosaurs, their forelegs were longer than their hind legs, and their shoulders were very high. This allowed the animals to reach up into the highest trees to feed on leaves, needles, and twigs.

The skull of *Brachiosaurus* has a huge space in the nose area, giving the head a domed appearance. *Macronarian* means big-nosed.

The Towering Giant

Brachiosaurus was one of the first macronarians to be discovered. Because scientists of the time didn't have enough information when fossils of other macronarians were found, they originally thought all of these animals were the same. However, we now know that while many of these discoveries were of creatures closely related to *Brachiosaurus*, they were actually different species. *Brachiosaurus* lived alongside *Diplodocus* and the other diplodocids in North America at the end of the Jurassic Period.

This huge macronarian in the Berlin museum was once thought to be a *Brachiosaurus*. It is now identified as a *Giraffatitan*.

CAMBRIAN	ORDOVICIAN	SILURIAN	DEVONIAN	CARBONIFEROUS	PERMIAN	TRIASSIC	JURASSIC	CRETACEOUS	CENOZOIC
							150 MYA		

Name: *Brachiosaurus* (*brak*-ee-oh-SORE-us)
Clade: Sauropoda
Length: Up to 72 ft. (22 m)
Weight: Up to 52 tn. (47 t)

ANIMAL PROFILE

A Long-Lived Family

The macronarians appeared in the middle of the Jurassic Period and survived until the age of dinosaurs came to a close with the end of the Cretaceous Period. During that time, they spread throughout the world and developed many strange shapes.

Europasaurus was a smaller macronarian. It was the size of a cow and lived on islands.

The tail of *Brachiosaurus* was quite short. It was used to balance the movement of the neck and head.

The legs were held straight like pillars to support the great weight of the animal.

DID YOU KNOW? Some scientists think the *Brachiosaurus* fossils we have are of specimens that were not fully grown. An adult *Brachiosaurus* may have been even bigger.

Camptosaurus

Besides sauropods, the other major group of plant-eating dinosaurs was ornithopods, or bird-footed dinosaurs. While sauropods supported their big bodies on all fours, most ornithopods could walk on their hind legs.

Like other ornithopods, *Camptosaurus* had a beak at the front of its mouth with cheeks at each side to hold plant material while it chewed.

A Fast Plant Eater

Camptosaurus was a common ornithopod from the late Jurassic Period. It usually walked on its hind legs and kept its hands free, so that it could gather food. Its food was any plant material it could reach. Judging from the wear on its tightly packed teeth, these plants were very tough. Since the ornithopod had strong hind legs, it could run away from the big meat eaters of the time.

Dryosaurus was a small, ostrich-sized ornithopod that lived alongside *Camptosaurus*.

Pigeon-Toed

The term bird-footed comes from the arrangement of the foot bones of these dinosaurs. In the 1800s, scientists thought the feet were like those of a bird. This distinguished them from the sauropods, which had toes similar to those of a lizard. Likewise, the theropods were believed to have toes similar to those of a mammal.

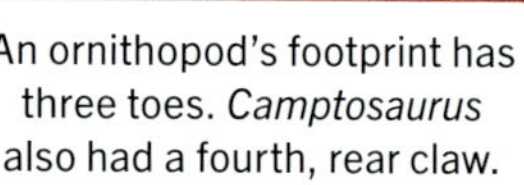
An ornithopod's footprint has three toes. *Camptosaurus* also had a fourth, rear claw.

CAMBRIAN | ORDOVICIAN | SILURIAN | DEVONIAN | CARBONIFEROUS | PERMIAN | TRIASSIC | JURASSIC (150 MYA) | CRETACEOUS | CENOZOIC

Name: *Camptosaurus* (*kamp*-toe-SORE-us)
Clade: Ornithopoda
Length: Up to 26 ft. (7.9 m)
Weight: Up to 2,000 lb. (900 kg)

ANIMAL PROFILE

DID YOU KNOW? *Camptosaurus* could probably run 15 miles per hour (24 kph).

Stegosaurus

Thyreophorans were dinosaurs protected by shields and plates. Stegosaurs were thyreophorans that had plates on their backs and spikes on their tails. Their plates were arranged vertically and ran in two rows down the neck, back, and tail.

The plates of *Stegosaurus* had a bony core and were covered with either skin or horn.

The Biggest and Showiest

With a double row of vertical plates down its back, two pairs of spikes on the end of its tail, and a tiny head, *Stegosaurus* is one of the most recognizable dinosaurs. It was also one of the biggest of the stegosaur group. From the side, it would have looked even bigger, with huge plates towering above the line of its back.

We have found many good fossils of *Stegosaurus*, so we know a lot about its skeleton.

Different Styles

All stegosaurs had two rows of back plates and spikes on their tails, but the arrangement of plates and spikes differed between individual species. The first stegosaurs appeared in the middle of the Jurassic Period in what is now China. They all died out by the middle of the Cretaceous, and their place in the ecosystem was taken by ankylosaurs.

Miragaia was a late Jurassic stegosaur from Portugal with a long neck like a sauropod.

Kentrosaurus, from late Jurassic East Africa, had more spines than plates. Its plates were small and narrow.

Name: *Stegosaurus* (*steg*-oh-SORE-us)
Clade: Thyreophora
Length: Up to 30 ft. (9 m)
Weight: Up to 5 tn. (4.5 t)

ANIMAL PROFILE

DID YOU KNOW? Scientists used to think that *Stegosaurus* had a second brain in its hips to control its hind legs and tail.

Archaeopteryx

The pterosaurs controlled the skies that birds would eventually take over. But in the Jurassic Period, birds were only just beginning to appear. They developed from small, meat-eating theropods. Because of this, many scientists regard birds as dinosaurs that have survived to the modern day.

The feathers on the arms of *Archaeopteryx* had the same shape and the overlapping pattern as the wings of many modern flying birds.

Early Bird

Archaeopteryx is widely regarded as the first bird. It had the bony tail, clawed hands, and toothy jaw of a small dinosaur, but it also had the wings and feathers of a bird. When its fossils were first discovered in the 1860s, they were used as proof that one kind of animal could evolve into another. *Archaeopteryx* was not the only birdlike creature of its time. Many other dinosaurs had features similar to birds.

Microraptor had flight feathers on its arms, legs, and tail. This small dinosaur could glide from tree to tree.

CAMBRIAN	ORDOVICIAN	SILURIAN	DEVONIAN	CARBONIFEROUS	PERMIAN	TRIASSIC	JURASSIC	CRETACEOUS	CENOZOIC
							150 MYA		

Name: *Archaeopteryx* (*ark*-ee-OPT-er-ix)
Order: Theropoda
Length: Up to 1.7 ft. (50 cm)
Weight: Up to 2.2 lb. (1 kg)

ANIMAL PROFILE

Iberomesornis could fly with its clawed wings. It had a more birdlike tail than *Archaeopteryx*.

Part Bird, Part Dinosaur

Feathers first appeared on small Jurassic theropods as insulation to keep the animals warm. It was only later that these feathers developed other purposes. Some feathers became big and showy and were used for display. Sometimes, these feathers could be used to catch the wind and help the animal run faster. Eventually, these became flight feathers.

Caudipteryx had showy feathers on its arms but could not fly.

Later birds had beaks instead of jaws, lost their wing claws, and developed stubby tails. All of these changes made them lighter than *Archaeopteryx* and helped them fly better.

DID YOU KNOW? *Archaeopteryx* is known from a dozen fossils, all found in the same quarry in southern Germany.

Camarasaurus

Four species of Camarasaurs lived in what is now North America toward the end of the Jurassic Period. The most famous, *Camarasaurus*, was first discovered in 1877. Since then, more than 500 specimens have been found in the United States, making the creature one of the most commonly excavated sauropods.

An Important Fossil

For many years, scientists disagreed about how sauropods walked. Some believed they walked with their legs under their bodies, while others thought they splayed their legs out like crocodiles. A *Camarasaurus* skeleton discovered in 1919 in Utah helped finally answer the question. The *Camarasaurus* had been fossilized with its front legs in place, proving it held them under its body.

This *Camarasaurus* skeleton was so complete that even the tiny bones of its inner ear were intact!

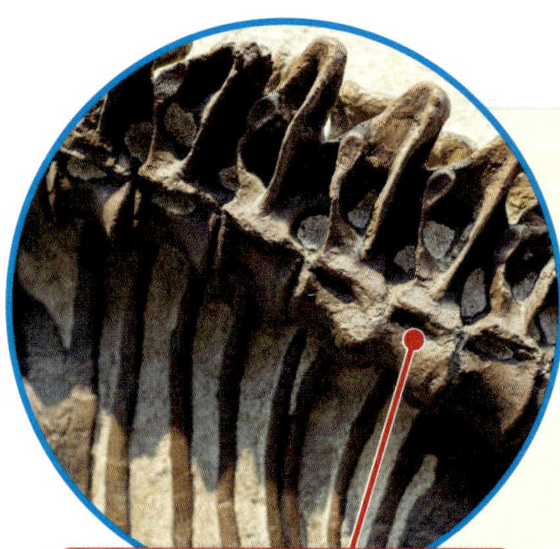

The empty spaces may have held air sacs, which could have been part of the dinosaur's respiratory system.

Hollow Backbones

The vertebrae of *Camarasaurus* were filled with pockets of empty space. This made the creature much lighter and likely helped it move around more easily. Many birds today have hollow bones, which helps make them light enough to fly.

CAMBRIAN ORDOVICIAN SILURIAN DEVONIAN CARBONIFEROUS PERMIAN TRIASSIC JURASSIC CRETACEOUS CENOZOIC

150 MYA

Name: *Camarasaurus* (kam-*ah*-ruh-SORE-us)

Class: Sauropoda

Length: Up to 75 ft. (23 m)

Weight: Up to 20 tn. (18 t)

ANIMAL PROFILE

The large, chisel-like teeth of *Camarasaurus* were stronger than those of other sauropods.

The short, boxy skull and powerful jaw muscles of *Camarasaurus* gave it enough bite force to chop up tough plants.

This dinosaur's body wasn't as long as other sauropods of its time, but it stood taller than most.

DID YOU KNOW? *Camarasaurus* is Greek for chambered lizard, referring to the empty chambers within its vertebrae.

Apatosaurus

Apatosaurus was one of the largest animals to live on Earth. It walked on enormous legs and towered over all other life during the late Jurassic Period. In fact, the sauropod was so large that some scientists have wondered if it occasionally swam to support its weight. So far, no evidence has been found to confirm this theory.

Apatosaurus **was too large to be prey for small predators, but it may have used its long tail to defend itself against larger ones.**

Apatosaurus vs. *Brontosaurus*

In the 1800s, scientists thought there were two very different species of apatosaurs, *Apatosaurus* and *Brontosaurus*. However, in 1903, paleontologist Elmer Riggs argued that the two were so similar they should be one species. Some modern scientists think that there are enough differences between the two creatures to separate them into two species once again, but not everyone agrees.

Brontosaurus skeletons are found in only North America, but *Apatosaurus* fossils have been found in both North America and Europe.

Skull Mix-Up

The first *Apatosaurus* skeleton ever assembled was put together in 1905. It had a skull that was square with a flat nose. However, scientists in 1978 discovered that the wrong skull had been added to the skeleton. They found the correct skull in the museum's storage. The true *Apatosaurus* skull was much longer and shaped like a cone.

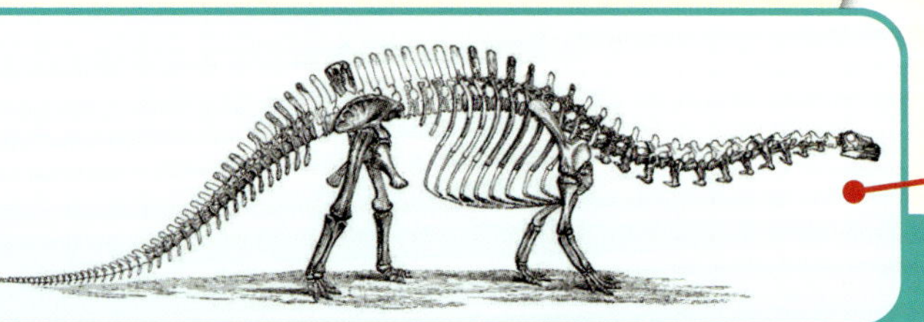

Apatosaurus fossils were first discovered during the Great Dinosaur Rush, when paleontologists competed to discover the most dinosaurs.

Name: *Apatosaurus* (ah-*pat*-uh-SORE-us)
Clade: Sauropoda
Length: Up to 75 ft. (23 m)
Weight: Up to 45 tn. (41 t)

DID YOU KNOW? Only one *Apatosaurus* skeleton has been discovered with the skull attached.

Agilisaurus

Plant-eating ornithopods lived on every continent during the Jurassic Period. One small and incredibly fast ornithopod, called *Agilisaurus,* lived in eastern Asia.

This dinosaur might have used its tail for balance when running.

Digging Up a Surprise

In 1984, workers building the Zigong Dinosaur Museum in Sichuan, China, uncovered the fossilized skeleton of an *Agilisaurus* dinosaur. It was one of the most complete small ornithopods ever discovered. So far, it is the only fossilized skeleton of *Agilisaurus* ever found.

The Zigong Dinosaur Museum was built over an open dig site. Visitors to the museum can see fossils still in the ground.

The *Agilisaurus* skeleton is on display in the museum where it was discovered.

Built for Running

The lower leg bones of *Agilisaurus* were longer than its upper leg bones. This suggests the dinosaur was bipedal, or able to run on two legs. The creature was also small and light, which probably made it very fast. It likely used its speed to escape from predators.

DID YOU KNOW? The dig site where the Zigong Dinosaur Museum was built has the largest cluster of dinosaur fossils from the Middle Jurassic ever discovered.

Compsognathus

Many Jurassic theropods were very large. But one theropod, *Compsognathus*, was one of the smallest dinosaurs that ever lived. Although it was only about the size of a turkey, *Compsognathus* had many of the same hunting adaptations as its larger dinosaur cousins. These included a mouth full of pointed teeth and fingers tipped with sharp claws.

Small but Fierce

Compsognathus probably ate small animals, such as reptiles, amphibians, and fish. It chased after prey at high speeds and snatched up meals with its claws and long snout. Some fossil specimens were found on islands and in areas that had lagoons, leading scientists to believe that *Compsognathus* may have been able to swim.

This *Compsognathus* skeleton was found with a small lizard meal in its belly.

Compsognathus balanced on its toes as it walked and ran.

A Fast Hunter

The hips and legs of *Compsognathus* were built for speed. Scientists think these dinosaurs may have been able to run at speeds of up to 40 mph (64 kph). That would have been fast enough to chase down almost any small prey.

DID YOU KNOW? Because of its forward-facing eyes, scientists think *Compsognathus* probably relied mostly on sight while hunting.

Europasaurus

While most sauropods were extremely large, *Europasaurus* was an exception. Scientists think that this maybe have been because it lived in an area with fewer food resources. With less to eat, it may not have been able to maintain a body as large as other sauropods.

Europasaurus is thought to have lived on an island near what is now Germany.

The Island Rule

Animals isolated on islands can grow or shrink over generations. Scientists call this the island rule. If there are few predators on an island, prey animals often grow bigger. But if there is less food, the animals may instead decrease in size over time. Paleontologists think *Europosaurus* lived on an island where it had less food than sauropods on the mainland, and so it became much smaller.

The tallest of *Europasaurus* stood about 10 ft. (3 m) high.

Europasaurus Shrinks

It's possible that rising sea levels trapped *Europasaurus*'s ancestors on an island. With fewer plants to eat, the dinosaur became smaller with each generation. The fossils of *Europasaurus* show that it grew more slowly than its relatives on the mainland, which may have also contributed to its smaller size.

Name: *Europasaurus* (yoo-*roh*-pah-SORE-us)

Class: Sauropoda

Length: Up to 20 ft. (6.2 m)

Weight: Up to 1,100 lb. (500 kg)

DID YOU KNOW? *Europasaurus* provided scientists with the first evidence that the island rule also applied to dinosaurs.

Allosaurus

Carnosaurs were a group of the fiercest predators of the Jurassic Period. Although it is possible some were scavengers that fed on dead animals, their bodies were made for hunting. Allosauroids were a group of large carnosaurs. Scientists have identified two species of *Allosaurus* so far, but there may have been even more.

Allosaurus may have hunted in small groups with other members of their species.

A Fearsome Predator

Allosaurus probably ate smaller dinosaurs. Its powerful legs made it faster than other carnosaurs of its time, and it was likely also faster than the dinosaurs it fed on. Powerful arms and large claws would have helped it attack prey.

A Head for Eating

The teeth of *Allosaurus* were up to 3 inches (7.6 cm) long and had sides that were serrated like steak knives. This helped it tear the flesh off its prey. The skull of *Allosaurus* was shaped so that even its back teeth could tear into its prey as it closed its jaws.

The Natural History Museum of Utah has the largest collection of *Allosaurus* fossils in the world.

Name: *Allosaurus* (*al*-oh-SORE-us)
Class: Theropoda
Length: Up to 35 ft. (10.5 m)
Weight: Up to 3 tn. (2.7 t)

ANIMAL PROFILE

DID YOU KNOW? Because so many of its fossils have been found in Utah, the *Allosaurus* has been named as the state fossil.

The Fossilized Past

The Jurassic Period lasted about 56.3 million years. At its start, sea levels were high, and Earth's climate was more tropical than it is today. But as the period progressed, sea levels dropped and the planet cooled. Paleontologists still study the fossils from this time to learn how life adapted to a changing planet.

The Morrison Formation

Much of what we know about Jurassic life in North America comes from the Morrison Formation, a layer of rock that is found under the western United States. Fossils from *Diplodocus*, *Apatosaurus*, *Stegosaurus*, *Allosaurus*, and more have been found there.

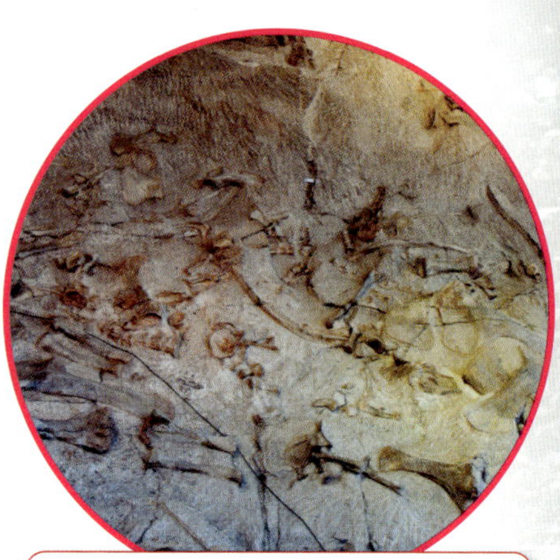

More than 200,000 acres of the Morrison Formation are protected as part of Dinosaur National Monument.

Footprints Found

New discoveries of Jurassic fossils continue to be made. In 2025, scientists realized a 200-million-year-old rock kept at an Australian high school held fossilized footprints from 47 different dinosaurs. It has the most dinosaur footprints of any fossil from Australia.

Changing Science

Paleontology started out as part of geology, the branch of science that studies how rock changes over time. While the first paleontologists mostly described and organized fossils, paleontologists today try to explain how prehistoric animals lived and behaved. New technology, such as DNA analysis, could help these scientists learn even more about the traits and habits of ancient creatures.

Review and Reflect

Now that you've read about life in the Jurassic Period, let's review what you've learned. Use the following questions to reflect on your newfound knowledge and integrate it with what you already knew.

Check for Understanding

1. What were the two main groups of plesiosaurs? *(See p. 6)*
2. How was *Geosaurus* adapted for life in the ocean? *(See p. 8)*
3. What evidence have scientists found that tells them pterosaurs walked on all fours? *(See p. 10)*
4. Why were the *Coelophysis* fossils found in New Mexico so well-preserved? *(See p. 14)*
5. What purpose do paleontologists think the two crests of *Dilophosaurus* could have served? *(See p. 17)*
6. What features made *Yangchuanosaurus* a successful hunter? *(See p. 18)*
7. How were macronarian dinosaurs different from diplodocids? *(See p. 22)*
8. Why was *Camptosaurus* able to walk on its hind legs? *(See p. 25)*
9. What are two theories for how *Stegosaurus* used its plates? *(See p. 27)*
10. What feature of Camarasaurus vertebrae made them lighter? *(See p. 30)*
11. When did scientists discover that the first *Apatosaurus* skeleton ever assembled had the wrong skull? *(See p. 32)*
12. Where was the only *Agilisaurus* fossil ever discovered found? *(See p. 34)*
13. What speed do scientists think *Compsognathus* could have reached? *(See p. 36)*
14. What theories do paleontologists have for why *Europasaurus* was much smaller than other sauropods? *(See p. 38)*
15. Where is the largest collection of *Allosaurus* fossils located? *(See p. 40)*

Making Connections

1. *Archaeopteryx* had features similar to both birds and dinosaurs. How did these differ from the features of the pterosaurs? How were they similar?
2. Compare the hunting strategies of *Allosaurus* and *Compsognathus*. How did size influence the way each hunted?
3. Plant eaters, such as *Stegosaurus*, and meat eaters, such as *Yangchuanosaurus*, had very different physical features. List a few and explain what these differences show us about how plant eaters and meat eaters adapted to one another during the Jurassic Period?
4. *Pterodactylus* had hollow bones that made flight possible. What other modern animals share this feature? How are they similar or dissimilar to *Pterodactylus*?
5. Choose one animal from this book and explain how its features helped it survive. Then, compare it with an animal alive today with similar features. Could they survive in each other's environments?

In Your Own Words

1. Which creature in this book do you think was the best adapted to its environment? Explain why.
2. If you could spend one day observing a group of dinosaurs in their natural environment, which ones would you pick and what would you want to learn about their behavior?
3. Pick a creature in this book and imagine it existed today. What modern environments might it survive in, and what challenges would it face?
4. Imagine you are a scientist studying *Liopleurodon*. What tools or methods would you use to learn more about it?
5. The island rule might explain why *Europasaurus* was much smaller than other sauropods. Can you think of a modern-day animal that may have been affected by the island rule in a similar way?

Glossary

Cambrian a geological period lasting from 541 to 485 million years ago

carnivore a meat-eating animal

clade a biological grouping of organisms that have a common ancestor

crest a growth of bones, scales, feathers, skin, or hair on the head or back of an animal

Cretaceous a geological period lasting from 145 to 66 million years ago

Devonian a geological period lasting from 419 to 355 million years ago

evolution the process by which a species changes and adapts over time

extinction when the last living member of an animal species has died

family a biological group smaller than a class but larger than a genus

fossil prehistoric remains that have become preserved in rock

insulation any material used to help keep something warm

Jurassic a geological period lasting from 201 to 145 million years ago

mammal an animal that gives birth to live young and feeds them milk

order a biological grouping that is smaller than a class but larger than a family

Permian a geological period lasting from 299 to 252 million years ago

plate a bony section on the outer body of a dinosaur

predator an animal that hunts and eats other animals

prey an animal that is hunted and eaten by other animals

quarry an open mine from which rock or other materials are extracted

reptile a scaly animal that is cold-blooded and usually lays eggs

species a biological group that is smaller than a genus and includes organisms that can produce offspring together

Triassic a geological period that lasted from 252 to 201 million years ago

vertebra a bone that is part of the spine

warm-blooded an animal that can control its own body temperature

Read More

Claybourne, Anna. *Paleontology (Science-ology).* New York: Rosen Publishing Group, 2026.

Drimmer, Stephanie. *How to Survive in the Age of Dinosaurs: A Handy Guide to Dodging Deadly Predators, Riding Out Mega-Monsoons, and Escaping Other Perils of the Prehistoric (How to Survive).* Washington, D.C.: National Geographic, 2023.

Hibbert, Clare. *Dinosaurs (Prehistoric Life).* New York: Gareth Stevens Publishing, 2023.

Martin, Claudia. *Exploring Fossils (Rocks & Fossils).* Minneapolis: Bearport Publishing, 2026.

Learn More Online

1. Go to **FactSurfer.com** or scan the QR code below.
2. Enter "**Warm Wet World**" into the search box.
3. Click on the cover of this book to see a list of websites.

Index